HOW TO
MEASURE
SURVEY
RELIABILITY
AND VALIDITY

THE SURVEY KIT

Purpose: The purposes of this 9-volume Kit are to enable readers to prepare and conduct surveys and become better users of survey results. Surveys are conducted to collect information by asking questions of people on the telephone, face-to-face, and by mail. The questions can be about attitudes, beliefs, and behavior as well as socioeconomic and health status. To do a good survey also means knowing how to ask questions, design the survey (research) project, sample respondents, collect reliable and valid information, and analyze and report the results. You also need to know how to plan and budget for your survey.

Users: The Kit is for students in undergraduate and graduate classes in the social and health sciences and for individuals in the public and private sectors who are responsible for conducting and using surveys. Its primary goal is to enable users to prepare surveys, and collect data that are accurate and useful for primarily practical purposes. Sometimes, these practical purposes overlap the objectives of scientific research and so survey researchers will also find the Kit useful.

Format of the Kit: All books in the series contain instructional objectives, exercises and answers, examples of surveys in use and illustrations of survey questions, guidelines for action, checklists of do's and don'ts, and annotated references.

Volumes in The Survey Kit:

1. **The Survey Handbook**
   Arlene Fink

2. **How to Ask Survey Questions**
   Arlene Fink

3. **How to Conduct Self-Administered and Mail Surveys**
   Linda B. Bourque and *Eve P. Fielder*

4. **How to Conduct Interviews by Telephone and in Person**
   James H. Frey and *Sabine Mertens Oishi*

5. **How to Design Surveys**
   Arlene Fink

6. **How to Sample in Surveys**
   Arlene Fink

7. **How to Measure Survey Reliability and Validity**
   Mark S. Litwin

8. **How to Analyze Survey Data**
   Arlene Fink

9. **How to Report on Surveys**
   Arlene Fink

THE SURVEY KIT 7

HOW TO MEASURE SURVEY RELIABILITY AND VALIDITY

MARK S. LITWIN

SAGE Publications
International Educational and Professional Publisher
Thousand Oaks London New Delhi

For information address:

SAGE Publications, Inc.
2455 Teller Road
Thousand Oaks, California 91320
E-mail: order@sagepub.com

SAGE Publications Ltd.
6 Bonhill Street
London EC2A 4PU
United Kingdom

SAGE Publications India Pvt. Ltd.
M-32 Market
Greater Kailash I
New Delhi 110 048 India

Printed in the United States of America

Library of Congress Cataloging-in-Publication Data

Main entry under title:

The survey kit.
    p. cm.
    Includes bibliographical references.
    Contents: v. 1. The survey handbook / Arlene Fink — v. 2. How to ask survey questions / Arlene Fink — v. 3. How to conduct self-administered and mail surveys / Linda B. Bourque, Eve P. Fielder — v. 4. How to conduct interviews by telephone and in person / James H. Frey, Sabine Mertens Oishi — v. 5. How to design surveys / Arlene Fink — v. 6. How to sample in surveys / Arlene Fink — v. 7. How to measure survey reliability and validity / Mark S. Litwin — v. 8. How to analyze survey data / Arlene Fink — v. 9. How to report on surveys / Arlene Fink.
    ISBN 0-8039-7388-8 (pbk. : The survey kit : alk. paper)
    1. Social surveys. 2. Health surveys. I. Fink, Arlene.
HN29.S724   1995
300′.723—dc20   95-12712

This book is printed on acid-free paper.

96 97 98 99 10 9 8 7 6 5 4 3 2

Sage Production Editor: Diane S. Foster
Sage Copy Editor: Joyce Kuhn
Sage Typesetter: Janelle LeMaster

Contents

How to Measure Survey Reliability and Validity: Learning Objectives

The aim of this book is to guide the reader in assessing and interpreting the quality of collected survey data by thoroughly examining the survey instrument used. Also presented are important considerations in coding and pilot-testing surveys. Specific objectives are to:

- Select and apply reliability criteria, including:

  - Test-retest reliability
  - Alternate-form reliability
  - Internal consistency reliability
  - Interobserver reliability
  - Intraobserver reliability

- Select and apply validity criteria, including:

  - Content validity
  - Criterion validity
  - Construct validity

- Understand the fundamental principles of scaling and scoring

- Create and use a codebook for survey data

- Pilot-test new and established surveys

- Address cross-cultural issues in survey research

1

Overview of Psychometrics

A successful data collection survey is not simply a set of well-designed questions that are written down and administered to a sample population. There are good surveys and bad ones. Bad surveys produce bad data, that is, data that are unreliable, irreproducible, or invalid or that waste resources. Conversely, good surveys yield critical information and provide important windows into the heart of the topic of interest.

Psychometrics is the branch of survey research that enables you to determine how good the survey is. It provides a way to quantify the precision of measurement of qualitative concepts, such as satisfaction. Example 1.1 presents two surveys of hotel guest satisfaction. It is not obvious whether one or the other is better, but they are clearly different. During the course of this book, you will learn how to evaluate their differences.

EXAMPLE 1.1
Two Surveys of Guest Satisfaction

Purpose of the Survey: To assess guest satisfaction at a downtown hotel with a three-item survey at the time of checkout

Survey 1: *Circle one number for each item*

1. Did you enjoy your stay?
   - Yes. 1
   - No. 2

2. How was the service at the hotel?
   - Good. 1
   - Bad 2

3. Would you stay here again?
   - Yes. 1
   - No. 2

Survey 2: *Circle one number for each item*

1. Overall, considering the service, food, and all other aspects of our hotel, how would you describe your stay here?

   - Very enjoyable. 1
   - Somewhat enjoyable. 2
   - Neither enjoyable nor unenjoyable 3
   - Somewhat unenjoyable 4
   - Very unenjoyable 5

2. How would you describe our service?

   More efficient than other hotels I have
   stayed in 1
   Equally efficient to other hotels I have
   stayed in 2
   Less efficient than other hotels I have
   stayed in 3

3. How likely are you to stay here again?

   Highly likely. 1
   Likely 2
   Not sure 3
   Unlikely 4
   Highly unlikely 5

Which survey is better? Survey 2 appears as though it might produce more useful information because it provides more than just the yes/no type questions used in Survey 1, but you really don't know quantitatively which survey is better. What exactly is meant by *better?* The better survey will more accurately measure guest satisfaction, producing more useful data from which to draw conclusions about the hotel's performance. Strictly speaking, it is difficult to assess the quality of the data you collect. It is easier to assess the accuracy of the survey instrument used to collect that data. This assessment consists primarily of looking at the *reliability* and the *validity* of the survey instrument. Example 1.2 demonstrates that different tools used to measure electrical resistance may produce completely different results. The only way to determine which, if either, is correct is by looking directly at the accuracy of the measurement tools.

EXAMPLE 1.2
Resistance Meters

Two licensed electricians use different resistance meters to measure the ohms in four brand-new circuits during a new product analysis. Pat uses the old meter she has been using for the last 15 years. Jerry uses a new model that he just bought from HomeLine, Inc., a reputable mail order company. After the measurements are taken, Pat's data are 6, 16, 38, and 119 ohms. Jerry's data are 19, 28, 73, and 184 ohms. Because there is no way to determine which, if either, data set is correct, the accuracy of the resistance meters themselves must be assessed. This is done by asking both Pat and Jerry to measure the resistance in a series of quality-control circuits, in which the ohmage is known with certainty in advance. After Pat and Jerry measure the resistance three different times in the quality-control circuits, Pat's meter is found to be more accurate. Therefore, we use her data in the new product analysis of the four new circuits.

The resistance meters in Example 1.2 demonstrate an important concept. Before a survey instrument can be used to collect meaningful data, you must test it to ensure its accuracy. This is true regardless of whether you are dealing with resistance meters, guest satisfaction questionnaires, crime surveys, depression scales, or any other survey instrument. What matters is not how quantitative the data are but how well the survey instrument performs. In the following chapters, this idea is explored in greater detail as the reliability and the validity of survey instruments are discussed.

2 Reliability

In any set of data you collect, there will be some amount of error. Naturally, you want to minimize this error so that the data provide a more accurate reflection of the truth.

In survey research, error comprises two components: random error and measurement error. **Random error** is the unpredictable error that occurs in all research. It may be caused by many different factors but is affected primarily by sampling techniques. To lower the chance of random error, you could select a larger and more representative sample. This increases the cost of the study, so it is often neither practical nor feasible simply to expand the sample. Instead, statistics are used to calculate the probability that a particular result is due to random error. If that probability falls below the limit you set, then you "reject the null hypothesis" and draw inferences about your population. Recall that in statistical analysis a conservative assumption, called the null hypothesis, is made that the two groups of interest do not differ in the particular variable being studied. For instance, in Example 1.1 (Chapter 1), if guest satisfaction between men and women was being compared, the null hypothesis would be that there is no difference. The survey research would be designed to try and reject that null hypothesis, thus allowing inferences to be drawn about differences between male and female hotel guests (for more information on hypothesis testing, see **How to Analyze Survey Data,** Vol. 8 in this series).

Measurement error refers to how well or poorly a particular instrument performs in a given population. No instrument is perfect, so you can expect some error to occur during the measurement process. For example, a stopwatch with a minute hand but no second hand cannot measure a runner's time in a 5-kilometer race to the nearest second. The best it can do is count minutes. Differences in the runner's time of less than 60 seconds will be lost in the measurement error of the stopwatch. The lower the measurement error, the closer the data are to the truth. However, even when random error is thought to be zero, some measurement error will occur. This measurement error reflects the precision (or lack of precision) of the survey instrument itself.

Reliability is a statistical measure of how reproducible the survey instrument's data are. Example 2.1 shows how two different tools used to measure fabric may have very different reliabilities.

EXAMPLE 2.1
Fabric Measurement

Honor Guard Fabric Company sells its fabric by the yard and uses expensive aluminum yardsticks to quantify the amount of each purchase. Dewey Bilkham Fabrics also sells its fabric by the yard but uses tape measures made from inexpensive thin rubber strips to measure its quantities. Fran needs exactly 3 yards of blue cotton fabric to make a slipcover for a favorite living room chair. At Dewey Bilkham, Fran has found over the years that the lengths of measured fabric are inconsistent. Because the rubber tape measures can be stretched to varying degrees depending on the strength of the salesperson, a measured yard may actually be anywhere from 35 inches to 41 inches. At Honor Guard, a measured yard of fabric is always the same length, varying only with the visual acuity of the salesperson. Therefore, Fran goes to Honor Guard to buy fabric, having learned that there a yard is always a yard.

The metal yardsticks are more reliable and have less measurement error than the rubber tape measures. Thus, Honor Guard's results are a more accurate reflection of the truth. Even so, there may still be some degree of measurement error. If the salesperson at Honor Guard doesn't see very well and cannot read the difference between 36 inches and 35 inches, then Fran may still get shorted. Neither the metal yardsticks nor the rubber tape measures are perfectly reliable, so there is always some possibility of measurement error.

No survey instrument or test is perfectly reliable, but some are clearly more reliable than others. When evaluating the value of a data set, begin by looking at the reliability characteristics of the measurement instrument.

Types of Reliability

Reliability is commonly assessed in three forms: test-retest, alternate-form, and internal consistency. Intraobserver and interobserver reliability are also addressed.

TEST-RETEST

Test-retest reliability is the most commonly used indicator of survey instrument reliability. It is measured by having the same set of respondents complete a survey at two different points in time to see how stable the responses are. It is a measure of how reproducible a set of results is. Correlation coefficients, or *r* **values,** are then calculated to compare the two sets of responses (see **How to Analyze Survey Data**, Vol. 8 in this series). These correlation coefficients are collectively referred to as the survey instrument's test-retest reliability. In general, *r* values are considered good if they equal or exceed 0.70. Sometimes, data are not collected from a group of subjects but are recorded by one observer. In this case, test-retest reliability is assessed by having that individual make two separate measurements. These two data sets from the same observer are then compared with each other. The correlation between two data sets from the same individual is commonly known as **intraobserver reliability.** It measures the stability of responses from the same respondent and is a form of test-retest reliability.

In Example 2.2, the measurement of test-retest reliability is demonstrated in a survey item that asks about grand larceny rates in urban centers.

EXAMPLE 2.2
Test-Retest Reliability of a Survey
Instrument Measuring Crime Rates

Ron has designed a new survey instrument to measure grand larceny rates in a group of urban centers at high risk for various types of crime. One of the items on the survey asks the deputy chief of police in each urban center whether grand larceny rates have been mild, moderate, or severe during the past month. To gauge whether respondents' answers to this item are consistent over time, Ron administers the survey instrument once to a sample of 50 deputy police chiefs in different urban centers and records the data. He then administers the identical survey instrument a second time 4 weeks later to the same 50 deputy police chiefs and records those data. Because actual grand larceny rates tend to be stable over short periods of time, Ron expects that any differences in the survey responses will reflect measurement error of the survey instrument and not actual changes in the crime rates. When Ron compares the sets of data from the two different time points, he finds that the correlation coefficient is 0.89. He knows that this item produces responses that are stable over moderate time periods. Therefore, his item has good test-retest reliability because it exceeds 0.70.

Example 2.3 presents a situation where test-retest reliability is low in a survey item that asks about energy levels in the same respondents described in Example 2.2.

EXAMPLE 2.3
Test-Retest Reliability of a
Survey Item Measuring Energy

Ron also wants to assess energy levels in the same deputy police chiefs to find out whether crime rates cause professional burnout among the officers. He designs an item that asks how fresh and energetic they feel today. He administers the same energy question at two time points 4 weeks apart but finds that for this item the correlation coefficient is only 0.32. Ron knows that this item does not produce responses that are stable over time because energy levels are much more likely to change from day to day and from week to week. Various factors may be influencing the changing responses. Perhaps energy levels are not dependent on crime rates in the urban centers. Perhaps energy levels are more related to salary or whether the chief had a chance to eat breakfast. Perhaps there are other factors influencing energy levels in this population. Because Ron does not know what these other factors are, he cannot control for them. Ron is forced to drop this energy item from his survey instrument. Its test-retest reliability is too low.

Test-retest reliability can be calculated not only for single items but also for groups of items. In fact, test-retest reliability is most often reported for entire survey instruments or for scales (more on scales later) within survey instruments. Example 2.4 demonstrates test-retest reliability in a series of written items administered together to measure pain in men undergoing hernia surgery.

EXAMPLE 2.4
Test-Retest Reliability of a Pain Scale

Jackie wants to measure postoperative pain in a group of 12 adult males undergoing hernia surgery. She designs a six-item pain assessment scale, with each item rated from 1 to 10, and then creates a scale score from the sum of the responses to these six items. She administers the survey instrument 2 hours after surgery (Time 1) and again 4 hours after surgery (Time 2), two points when pain levels should be similar. She then compares the two sets of pain scale scores by calculating a correlation coefficient and finds it to be 0.78. She concludes that her pain scale has good test-retest reliability during the immediate postoperative period in this population.

When measuring test-retest reliability, you must be careful not to select items or scales that measure variables likely to change over short periods of time. Variables that are likely to change over a given period of time will produce low test-retest reliability in measurement instruments. This does not indicate that the survey instrument is performing poorly but simply that the attribute itself has changed. Example 2.5 illustrates how to select an appropriate time interval over which to assess test-retest reliability.

EXAMPLE 2.5
Test-Retest Reliability of
Time Intervals in a Survey Instrument
Measuring Anxiety: Two Designs

Design 1

Eric uses a well-known short survey instrument to measure anxiety in a group of college students before and after midterm examinations. He administers the items 4 days prior to the exam (Time 1), 3 days prior to the exam (Time 2), and 2 days after the exam (Time 3). He calculates the correlation coefficient between Times 1 and 2 to be 0.84, the correlation coefficient between Times 1 and 3 to be 0.12, and the correlation coefficient between Times 2 and 3 to be 0.09. The correct test-retest reliability figure to report is 0.84. This reflects the stability of the responses to the survey instrument during a period when Eric would expect the responses to remain fairly stable. Eric deduces that the other two figures represent true changes in anxiety levels and not poor test-retest reliability. Based on his reliable survey instrument, he concludes that anxiety levels go down after exams.

Design 2

Bryan designs his own survey instrument to measure anxiety in the same group of college students at the same time points. His correlation coefficients are 0.34, 0.43, and 0.50, respectively, for Times 1, 2, and 3. Bryan cannot make any sound deductions about anxiety levels because his survey instrument does not have good test-retest reliability.

You can certainly measure characteristics that tend to change over time, but test-retest reliability must be documented over shorter periods to decrease the degree of measurement error attributable to the test itself. When measuring test-retest reliability, you must consider that individuals may become familiar with the items and simply answer based on their memory of what they answered the last time. This is called the **practice effect** and is a challenging problem to address in measures of test-retest reliability over short periods of time. It can falsely inflate test-retest reliability figures.

ALTERNATE-FORM

Alternate-form reliability provides one way to escape the problem of the practice effect. It involves using differently worded items to measure the same attribute. Questions and responses are reworded or their order changed to produce two items that are similar but not identical. You must be careful to create items that address the same exact aspect of behavior with the same vocabulary level and the same level of difficulty. Items must differ *only* in their wording. Items or scales are administered to the same population at different time points, and correlation coefficients are again calculated. If these are high, the survey instrument or item is said to have good alternate-form reliability. One common way to test alternate-form reliability is simply to change the order of the response set. In Example 2.6, two differently ordered response sets are presented for the same item question. Either response set can be used without changing the meaning of the question.

EXAMPLE 2.6
Alternate-Form Reliability
of Response Sets for Depression

The following are equivalent but differently ordered response sets to single items on depression. For each of these three items, the two response sets differ only in their sequence. They are good items for this method of measuring alternate-form reliability.

Item 1: Circle one number in each response set

Version A:

How often during the past 4 weeks have you felt sad and blue?

All of the time	1
Most of the time	2
Some of the time	3
Occasionally	4
Never	5

Version B:

How often during the past 4 weeks have you felt sad and blue?

Never	1
Occasionally	2
Some of the time	3
Most of the time	4
All of the time	5

Item 2: Circle one number in each response set

Version A:

During the past 4 weeks, I have felt downhearted:

Every day 1
Some days. 2
Never 3

Version B:

During the past 4 weeks, I have felt downhearted:

Never 1
Some days. 2
Every day 3

Item 3: Circle one number in each response set

Version A:

During the past 4 weeks, have you felt like hurting yourself?

Yes. 1
No. 2

Version B:

During the past 4 weeks, have you felt like hurting yourself?

No. 1
Yes. 2

Changing the order of the response set is most effective when the two time points are close together. This approach forces the respondent to read the items and response sets very carefully, thereby decreasing the practice effect. Another way to test alternate-form reliability is to change the wording of the response sets without changing the meaning. In Example 2.7, two items on urinary function are presented, each with two different response sets that collect the same information with different but synonymous wording.

EXAMPLE 2.7
Alternate-Form Reliability of
Response Set Wording on Urinary Function

The following are equivalent but differently worded response sets to two single items on urinary function. The response sets for each item are differently worded but functionally equivalent. This makes them good candidates for use in a test of alternate-form reliability.

Item 1: Circle one number in each response set

Version A:

During the past week, how often did you usually empty your bladder?

1 to 2 times per day	1
3 to 4 times per day	2
5 to 8 times per day	3
12 times per day.	4
More than 12 times per day.	5

Version B:

During the past week, how often did you usually empty your bladder?

Every 12 to 24 hours 1
Every 6 to 8 hours 2
Every 3 to 5 hours 3
Every 2 hours 4
More than every 2 hours 5

Item 2: *Circle one number in each response set*

Version A:

During the past 4 weeks, how much did you leak urine?

Never 1
A little bit. 2
A moderate amount. 3
A lot 4
Constantly 5

Version B:

During the past 4 weeks, how much did you leak urine?

I used no pads in my underwear 1
I used 1 pad per day 2
I used 2 to 3 pads per day 3
I used 4 to 6 pads per day 4
I used 7 or more pads per day 5

Another common method to test alternate-form reliability is to change the actual wording of the items themselves. Again, you must be very careful to design items that are truly equivalent to each other. Items that are worded with different degrees of difficulty do not measure the same attribute. They are more likely to measure the reading comprehension or cognitive function of the respondent. Example 2.8 demonstrates two questions that are *not* equivalent even though they are about the same topic. The items in this example would not provide a good test of alternate-form reliability.

EXAMPLE 2.8
Nonequivalent Item Rewording

The following are differently worded versions of the same item intended to measure assertiveness at work. If you look closely at the wording, you see that they do indeed ask basically the same question. In fact, the response sets are identical. But they are clearly *not* equivalent because their vocabulary levels are profoundly different. They would *not* be good items with which to test alternate-form reliability. The first is a measure of assertiveness, whereas the second is more a measure of reading comprehension.

Item 1: Circle one number

When your boss blames you for something you did not do, how often do you stick up for yourself?

          All of the time 1
          Some of the time 2
          None of the time 3

Item 2: *Circle one number*

When presented with difficult professional situations where a superior censures you for an act for which you are not responsible, how frequently do you respond in an assertive way?

> All of the time 1
> Some of the time 2
> None of the time 3

Despite the same response sets, these two versions are *not* equivalent and therefore *cannot* be used to test alternate-form reliability.

Example 2.9 illustrates two questions that are also differently worded but *are* equivalent and can be used to test alternate-form reliability. Notice that even though the response sets are different, the items are much closer than those shown in Example 2.8.

EXAMPLE 2.9
Equivalent Item Rewording

The following are equivalent but differently worded items that assess loneliness. Notice that although the items are different, they ask about the exact same issue in very similar ways. A high correlation coefficient, or *r* value, between the responses to these two items would indicate that the item has good alternate-form reliability.

Item 1: Circle one number

How often in the past month have you felt all alone in the world?

Every day 1
Some days 2
Occasionally. 3
Never 4

Item 2: Circle one number

During the past 4 weeks, how often have you felt a sense of loneliness?

All of the time 1
Sometimes 2
From time to time 3
Never 4

Although the items are worded differently and have different response sets, they effectively measure the same attribute—loneliness.

When testing alternate-form reliability, the different forms may be administered at separate time points to the same population. Alternatively, if the sample is large enough, it can be divided in half and each alternate form administered to half of the group. Results from the two halves are then compared with each other. This technique, called the **split halves method,** is generally accepted as being as good as administering the different forms to the same sample at different time points.

When using the split halves method, you must make sure to select the half-samples randomly. You must also measure the sociodemographic characteristics of both half-samples to make sure there are no group differences that might account for any disparities in the two data sets.

Although all of the preceding examples used two sets of wording or two response sets or two half-samples, there is no rule that limits the number to two. If your sample is large enough, you can use three, four, or more subsamples to test alternate forms of an item. You must check your sample sizes to make sure you have enough statistical power to show a difference in the alternate forms (for an explanation of statistical power, see **How to Analyze Survey Data,** Vol. 8 in this series).

INTERNAL CONSISTENCY

Internal consistency reliability is another commonly used psychometric measure in assessing survey instruments and scales. It is applied not to single items but to groups of items that are thought to measure different aspects of the same concept. Internal consistency is an indicator of how well the different items measure the same issue. This is important because a group of items that purports to measure one variable should indeed be clearly focused on that variable. Although single items may be quicker and less expensive to administer, the data set is richer and more reliable if several different items are used to gain information about a particular behavior or topic. Example 2.10 contains a real scale that is used in medical survey research today. It has been shown to have very high internal consistency reliability.

EXAMPLE 2.10
A Physical Function Scale

In the RAND Medical Outcomes Study (MOS), a large research project conducted in the 1980s, a series of items was developed to measure quality of life in patients with various medical conditions. The most popular survey instrument produced in the MOS is the RAND 36-Item Health Survey, alternatively known as Short Form 36, or SF-36. One of the eight dimensions measured in this survey instrument is physical function. Instead of simply choosing one item to assess physical function, the study's authors determined that it was more useful to ask 10 questions about physical function, as shown below.

Scale for Physical Function

The following questions are about activities you might do during a typical day. Does your health now limit you in these activities? If so, how much?

Circle one number on each line

	Limited a Lot	Limited a Little	Not Limited at All
1. **Vigorous activities**, such as running, lifting heavy objects, participating in strenuous sports	1	2	3
2. **Moderate activities**, such as moving a table, pushing a vacuum cleaner, bowling, or playing golf	1	2	3
3. Lifting or carrying groceries	1	2	3
4. Climbing **several** flights of stairs	1	2	3
5. Climbing **one** flight of stairs	1	2	3
6. Bending, kneeling, or stooping	1	2	3
7. Walking **more than a mile**	1	2	3
8. Walking **several blocks**	1	2	3
9. Walking **one block**	1	2	3
10. Bathing or dressing yourself	1	2	3

It is easy to see how this series of items provides much more information on physical function than a single item, such as the following:

Circle one number for the following item

	Limited a Lot	Limited a Little	Not Limited at All
How limited are you in your day-to-day physical activities?	1	2	3

Internal consistency is measured by calculating a statistic known as Cronbach's coefficient alpha, named for the 20th-century psychometrician who first reported it in 1951. Coefficient alpha measures internal consistency reliability among a group of items combined to form a single scale. It is a statistic that reflects the homogeneity of the scale. That is, it is a reflection of how well the different items complement each other in their measurement of different aspects of the same variable or quality. The formula can be found in any textbook of test theory or psychometric statistics (see also **How to Analyze Survey Data**, Vol. 8 in this series). Example 2.11 provides a demonstration of coefficient alpha calculation. For simplicity, the example contains a scale with three yes/no items, but coefficient alpha can also be calculated for longer scales containing items with more than two responses.

EXAMPLE 2.11
Calculating Internal Consistency

In the RAND 36-Item Health Survey, emotional health is assessed with five items. Suppose we created a smaller mental health scale consisting of the following subset of three items and wanted to test its internal consistency.

Circle one number on each line

During the past month:	Yes	No
Have you been a very nervous person? 1		0
Have you felt downhearted and blue? 1		0
Have you felt so down in the dumps that nothing could cheer you up? 1		0

The response set for each of these items results in a number of points that are summed to form the scale score. A low score reflects poorer emotional health, and a higher score indicates better emotional health. For simplicity, the response sets have been reduced to yes/no answers, with yes = 1 point and no = 0 points.

To calculate coefficient alpha, the scale is administered to a sample of 5 nursing home patients, with the following results obtained:

Patient	Item 1	Item 2	Item 3	Summed Scale Score
1	0	1	1	2
2	1	1	1	3
3	0	0	0	0
4	1	1	1	3
5	1	1	0	2
Percentage positive	3/5 = .6	4/5 = .8	3/5 = .6	

First, you must calculate the sample mean and the sample variance. (These formulas can be found in **How to Analyze Survey Data**, Vol. 8 in this series) Also note the percentage positive responses for each item and that the number of items in the scale is 3.

Calculations

The sample mean score is $(2 + 3 + 0 + 3 + 2)/5 = 2$.

The sample variance is

$$\frac{(2-2)^2 + (3-2)^2 + (0-2)^2 + (3-2)^2 + (2-2)^2}{(5-1)} = \frac{6}{4} = 1.5.$$

Coefficient alpha for a series of dichotomous items is

$$\left[1 - \frac{(\% \text{ positive})_i (\% \text{ negative})_i}{\text{Sample variance}} \right] \left[\frac{k}{k-1} \right],$$

where k = number of items in the scale.

Coefficient alpha is

$$\left[1 - \frac{1 - (.6)(.4) + (.8)(.2) + (.6)(.4)}{1.5} \right] \left[3/3 - 1 \right] = 0.86.$$

The internal consistency coefficient alpha of 0.86 suggests very good reliability in this scale of three dichotomous items.

In Example 2.11, coefficient alpha was calculated for a simple scale of three yes/no items. Most scales contain more than three items, each of which has more than two responses. Coefficient alpha can be calculated for these scales, too, but it is greatly facilitated by a good statistician and a computer.

If a scale's internal consistency reliability is low, it can often be improved by adding more items or by reexamining the existing items for clarity.

Reliability testing of items and scales provides quantitative measurements of how well an instrument performs in a given population. If you develop a new survey instrument, it is imperative to test it for reliability before using it to collect data from which you will draw inferences. One of the major drawbacks of new survey instruments is that they are often nothing more than collections of questions that seem to the surveyors to fit well together. Even when using established survey instruments with long and successful track records, it is important to calculate internal consistency reliability and, if possible, test-retest reliability to document its performance in your population. Established survey instruments typically undergo extensive psychometric evaluation; however, the author's sample population may be quite different from yours. When multicultural issues or language barriers are relevant considerations, it is especially important to conduct reliability testing. If you are collecting data from a group of subjects in whom that survey instrument has not previously been used, you must document the consistency of its psychometric properties, including reliability.

INTEROBSERVER

Interobserver (interrater) **reliability** provides a measure of how well two or more evaluators agree in their assessment of a variable. It is usually reported as a correlation coefficient between different data collectors. When survey instruments are self-administered by the respondent and designed to measure his or her own behaviors or attitudes, interobserver reliability is not used. However, whenever there is a subjective component in the measurement of an external variable, it is important to calculate this statistic. Sometimes, interobserver reliability is used as a psychometric property of a survey instrument; at other times, it is itself the variable of interest. Example 2.12 demonstrates the measurement of interobserver reliability in a survey designed to measure efficiency in the workplace.

EXAMPLE 2.12
Interobserver Reliability of a Survey Instrument Measuring the Impact of Job Sharing

Marlene designs a survey instrument to assess the impact of a new job-sharing policy at a newspaper production plant. The policy allows employees with small children to share a 40-hour work-week to allow each worker more time at home. The survey instrument is a questionnaire completed by a "peer judge," who answers a series of 20 questions on the efficiency of the 100-member workforce on each shift. Marlene plans to ask three different workers to act as peer judges and complete the survey instrument by quietly making observations during a regular shift. Marlene will calculate the efficiency score as determined by each peer judge and will then compare the three data sets by calculating correlation coefficients to determine the interobserver reliability of the survey instrument. If the correlations are high, Marlene will know that her survey instrument has high reliability from one observer to another. She may conclude that it can be used by various peer judges to measure the impact of the new policy on efficiency in this workforce. If the correlations are low, Marlene must consider that the survey instrument may be operator dependent, not a good quality for such a survey. She may then conclude that the survey instrument is not stable among different judges. She may decide to assess the new policy's impact by using one judge for all of the work shifts.

In another illustration, Example 2.13 demonstrates that interobserver reliability may be more than a psychometric statistic. It may also be the primary variable of interest.

EXAMPLE 2.13
Interobserver Reliability of a
Research Project on Mammography

Russell is very interested in determining whether mammography is a good test to diagnose early-stage breast cancer. He designs a research project in which he shows the same 10 mammograms to a series of 12 different radiologists. He will ask each radiologist individually to rate each mammogram as suspicious for cancer, indeterminant, or not suspicious for cancer. He will then compare the responses from the 12 radiologists with each other and calculate correlation coefficients. This will provide a measure of interobserver reliability. If the correlations are high, he will conclude that mammography has a high degree of interobserver reliability, but if they are low, he will conclude that the reliability of mammography is suspect. Russell plans to report his findings in the medical literature.

In this example, interobserver reliability is not only a psychometric property of the test but is also an outcome variable of primary interest to the data collector.

Interobserver reliability is often used when the measurement process is less quantitative than the variable being measured. The other forms of reliability previously discussed are more often used when the variable itself is more qualitative. There are, of course, exceptions to this general rule.

Reliability Recap

The following table summarizes the types of reliability and their characteristics along with comments on their use.

Type of Reliability	Characteristics	Comments
Test-retest	Measures the stability of responses over time, typically in the same group of respondents	Requires administration of survey to a sample at two different and appropriate points in time. Time points that are too far apart may produce diminished reliability estimates that reflect actual change over time in the variable of interest.
Intraobserver	Measures the stability of responses over time in the same individual respondent	Requires completion of a survey by an individual at two different and appropriate points in time. Time points that are too far apart may produce diminished reliability estimates that reflect actual change over time in the variable of interest.
Alternate-form	Uses differently worded stems or response sets to obtain the same information about a specific topic	Requires two items in which the wording is different but aimed at the same specific variable and at the same vocabulary level
Internal consistency	Measures how well several items in a scale vary together in a sample	Usually requires a computer to carry out calculations
Interobserver	Measures how well two or more respondents rate the same phenomenon	May be used to demonstrate reliability of a survey or may itself be the variable of interest in a study

Reliability is usually expressed as a correlation coefficient, or r value, between two sets of data. Levels of 0.70 or more are generally accepted as representing good reliability.

3 Validity

Besides determining a survey item's or scale's reliability, you must assess its **validity**, or how well it measures what it sets out to measure. An item that is supposed to measure pain should measure pain and not some related variable (e.g., anxiety). A scale that claims to measure emotional quality of life should not measure depression, a related but different variable. Reliability assessments are necessary, but they are not sufficient when examining the psychometric properties of a survey instrument. Once you document that a scale is reliable over time and in alternate forms, you must then make sure that it is reliably measuring the truth.

Example 3.1 takes another look at the problem of measuring fabric that was explored in Chapter 2's Example 2.1. Before, your concern was with reliability, but now you are concerned with validity.

EXAMPLE 3.1
Fabric Measurement Revisited

Recall from Example 2.1 that Honor Guard Fabric Company uses expensive aluminum yardsticks to measure the length of each piece of fabric it sells. You previously determined that these metal yardsticks are very reliable because they measure out the exact same length of cloth every time. Suppose that during a store audit Honor Guard finds that each of its 1-yard measuring sticks is actually 40 inches long. Every single time the clerk sells a yard of fabric, the measuring sticks reliably count out 40 inches of fabric. Over the years, the company realizes that it has given away thousands of inches of extra fabric because its expensive aluminum measuring sticks are too long. The measurement instruments are reliable but not valid.

Validity must be documented when evaluating new survey instruments or when applying established survey instruments to new populations. It is an important measure of a survey instrument's accuracy.

Types of Validity

Several types of validity are typically measured when assessing the performance of a survey instrument: face, content, criterion, and construct.

FACE

Face validity is based on a cursory review of items by untrained judges, such as your sister, boyfriend, or squash partner. Assessing face validity might involve simply showing your survey to a few untrained individuals to see whether they think the items look OK to them. It is the least scientific measure of all the validity measures and is often confused with content validity. Although the two are similar, face validity is a much more casual assessment of item appropriateness. In fact, many researchers do not consider face validity a measure of validity at all.

CONTENT

Content validity is a subjective measure of how appropriate the items seem to a set of reviewers who have some knowledge of the subject matter. The assessment of content validity typically involves an organized review of the survey's contents to ensure that it includes everything it should and does not include anything it shouldn't. When examining the content validity of medical scales, for example, it is important that actual patients and their families be included in the evaluation process. Clinicians may be unaware of the subtle nuances experienced by patients who live day-to-day with a medical condition. Families also may provide helpful insights into dimensions that might otherwise be overlooked by "experts." This said, it remains important for clinicians to review the items for relevance to and focus on the variables of interest. Content validity is not quantified with statistics. Rather, it is presented as an overall opinion of a group of trained judges. Strictly speaking, it is not a scientific measure of a survey instrument's accuracy. Nevertheless, it provides a good foundation on which to build a methodologically rigorous assessment of a survey instrument's validity.

In Example 3.2, content validity is assessed for a sociological survey on interactions between spouses.

EXAMPLE 3.2
Content Validity of a
Marital Interaction Scale

Josh designs a new scale to collect data on marital interaction as a dimension of health-related quality of life. He develops a series of 16 items about spousal communication, interpersonal confidence, and discussions within the marriage. He plans to use his new scale to assess the impact of social support on a large population of married cancer patients undergoing a difficult and stressful chemotherapy protocol.

Before administering his new scale, Josh asks 15 individuals— 3 oncologists, 3 psychologists, 2 social workers, 1 oncology nurse practitioner, 4 cancer patients, and 2 spouses of cancer patients— to review each of the items. He asks these reviewers to rate each item and the scale as a whole for appropriateness and relevance to the issue of marital interaction. He also asks each reviewer to list any areas that are pertinent to marital interaction but not covered in the 16 items. Once all the reviews are complete, Josh studies them to determine whether his new survey instrument has content validity.

If he had wished to assess face validity, Josh might have asked his college roommate or his mother to take a look at the survey and tell him whether the items seemed appropriate. Josh decides to bypass face validity because he has chosen to look more carefully at content validity and knows that face validity is basically worthless.

CRITERION

Criterion validity is a measure of how well one instrument stacks up against another instrument or predictor. It provides much more quantitative evidence on the accuracy of a survey instrument. It may be measured differently, depending on how much published literature is available in the area of study. Criterion validity may be broken down into two components: concurrent and predictive.

Concurrent

Concurrent validity requires that the survey instrument in question be judged against some other method that is acknowledged as a "gold standard" for assessing the same variable. It may be a published psychometric index, a scientific measurement of some factor, or another generally accepted test. The fundamental requirement is that it be regarded as a good way to measure the same concept. The statistic is calculated as a correlation coefficient with that test. A high correlation suggests good concurrent validity. Alternatively, a test may be selected for comparison that is expected to measure an attribute or behavior that is opposite to the dimension of interest. In this case, a low correlation indicates good concurrent validity. The reason why you would not use the established gold standard as your measure of choice is that it may be too cumbersome, expensive, or invasive to apply.

Example 3.3 demonstrates the use of an established scale to assess concurrent validity in a new scale.

EXAMPLE 3.3
Concurrent Validity of
a Pain Tolerance Index

Alisha develops a new four-item index to assess pain tolerance in a group of patients scheduled for surgery. The items draw information from patients' memory of their past experiences with pain. The results from the four items are summed to form a Pain Tolerance Index score. The higher the score, the greater the tolerance for pain. Her index is self-administered and takes about 1 minute for patients to complete. To assess concurrent validity, Alisha administers her four items together with a published pain tolerance survey instrument that has been in use for more than a decade in anesthesiology research. It contains 45 items, requires an interviewer, and takes an average of 1 hour to complete. It is also scored as a sum of item responses. It is generally accepted as the gold standard in the field.

Alisha uses both survey instruments to gather data from a sample of 24 patients. Alisha calculates the correlation coefficient to be 0.92 between the two tests of pain tolerance. She concludes that her index has high concurrent validity with the gold standard. Because hers is much shorter and easier to administer, she convinces the principal investigator in a large national study of postoperative pain to use her more efficient index. Alisha publishes her findings and is awarded a generous academic scholarship as a result of her work.

In Example 3.4, a new survey instrument's validity in measuring water supply is assessed by comparing it with a more standard measure of water supply.

EXAMPLE 3.4
Concurrent Validity of
a Water Supply Index

Luis develops an index of overall water supply in desert towns. It is a number calculated from a mathematical formula based on average monthly town rainfall, average monthly depth of the town reservoir, and average monthly water pressure in the kitchen of the local elementary school. The higher the index, the greater the water supply in the town. Luis collects data for 12 consecutive months and uses his formula to calculate a water supply index. During that year, he also records the number of days each month that the Department of Water declares as drought days. At the end of the year, Luis plots his index against the number of drought days for each month. He calculates the correlation coefficient between the two data sets to be -0.81. Because he reasons that these two variables should have an inverse relationship, Luis concludes that his index has good criterion validity.

Although it is important to evaluate concurrent validity, you must make sure to select a gold standard test that is truly a good criterion against which to judge your new survey instrument. It is not helpful to show good correlations with some obscure index just because it happens to be published in a journal or book. Always select gold standards that are relevant, well known, and accepted as being good measures of the variable of interest. When testing concurrent validity, select gold standards that have been demonstrated to have psychometric properties of their own. Otherwise, you will be comparing your new scales to a substandard criterion.

Predictive

Predictive validity is the ability of a survey instrument to forecast future events, behaviors, attitudes, or outcomes. It may be used during the course of a study to predict response to a stimulus, election winners, success of an intervention, time to a clinical endpoint, or other objective criteria. Over a brief interval, predictive validity is similar to concurrent validity in that it involves correlating the results of one test with the results of another administered around the same time. If the time frame is longer and the second test occurs much later, then the assessment is of predictive validity. Like concurrent validity, predictive validity is calculated as a correlation coefficient between the initial test and the secondary outcome.

Example 3.5 demonstrates that the Pain Tolerance Index that was tested for concurrent validity in Example 3.3 may also be tested for predictive validity.

EXAMPLE 3.5
Predictive Validity of
the Pain Tolerance Index

Fourteen years after her initial success, Alisha from Example 3.3 becomes a professor of gynecology at a well-respected research university. She decides to use her Pain Tolerance Index to predict narcotic requirement in patients undergoing a hysterectomy. Having tested her index for reliability and concurrent validity, she now wants to test it for predictive validity. She administers the index to 24 of her preoperative patients and calculates an index score for each individual. Recall that a high score reflects a high tolerance for pain.

Once all the surgeries have been completed, Alisha reviews the medical records. She notes the number of doses of narcotic that were administered for postoperative pain control in each patient. She then calculates a correlation coefficient between the two data elements: index score and number of narcotic doses. When she finds that, the statistic is –0.84. As expected, there is a strong inverse correlation between the Pain Tolerance Index and the amount of narcotic required after surgery. Alisha is pleased to find that her index has high predictive validity in clinical practice. She publishes her results in a national medical journal and is later promoted to the position of chairperson of the gynecology department at the university.

Continuing with this theme, predictive validity can be used in a variety of settings to measure the accuracy of a survey instrument. One of the most well-known survey instruments is the Scholastic Aptitude Test (SAT). In Example 3.6, the SAT is used on a population of college students to predict academic success.

EXAMPLE 3.6
Predictive Validity of SAT Scores

Bob is the dean of students at Brook College, a small liberal arts school in Arizona, and decides to look into whether the SAT scores of entering freshmen predict how well the students will perform during their first semester at Brook. The dean looks back into the registrar's records for the past 5 years and gathers two data elements for each freshman: SAT score and first-semester grade point average. The dean enters the two data sets into his laptop computer and calculates a correlation coefficient between the two. To his surprise, he finds the statistic to be 0.45. The students' SAT scores do not appear to have high predictive validity for early success at Brook College. He immediately writes a memo to the dean of admissions asking that evaluation policies be revised to reflect this important new information.

When Jackie, the dean of admissions at Brook, receives Bob's memo, she decides to do a little investigating of her own. She takes Bob's data and breaks them down year by year. Using the same formula, she calculates correlation coefficients with her own laptop computer and finds that over the past 5 years the predictive validity of SAT scores has been 0.21, 0.36, 0.39, 0.57, and 0.72. Jackie writes a memo back to Bob, suggesting that although SAT scores did not previously have much predictive validity, they have become increasingly more useful in recent years. Jackie proudly sends a copy of her memo to the chancellor for consideration in her upcoming decision on who should be promoted to provost.

Predictive validity is one of the most important ways to measure a test's accuracy in practical applications; however, it is seldom used in longitudinal medical experiments that rely on surveys. Because the time frames are often several years long in such trials, secondary interventions may be implemented during the trial to alter the course of a disease or medical condition. If the final outcomes were compared with a test score from the start of the study, their correlation may be diminished. This would falsely decrease the measured predictive validity of the test and perhaps call into question the statistical qualities of an otherwise valid survey instrument.

Example 3.6 about SAT scores demonstrates that predictive validity (or any other psychometric statistic) may be used in various ways to support different hypotheses. You must be careful with the conclusions you draw from any of these measured psychometric properties. A good exercise is to ask peers in your area who are unfamiliar with your hypothesis to look at a summary of your data and draw conclusions. If enough people draw the same conclusion, you may be somewhat reassured that your inferences are correct. You may also ask peers to take your data and statistics and try to support a point that is opposite to your conclusions. This may open up your mind to different interpretations. It may unhinge your argument, or it may guide your approach to collecting more irrefutable evidence.

CONSTRUCT

Construct validity is the most valuable yet most difficult way of assessing a survey instrument. It is difficult to understand, to measure, and to report. This form of validity is often determined only after years of experience with a survey instrument. It is a measure of how meaningful the scale or survey instrument is when in practical use. Often, it is not calculated as a quantifiable statistic. Rather, it is frequently seen as a gestalt of how well a survey instrument performs in a multitude of settings and populations over a number of years. Construct validity is often thought to comprise two other forms of validity: convergent and divergent.

Convergent

Convergent validity implies that several different methods for obtaining the same information about a given trait or concept produce similar results. Evaluating convergent validity is analogous to measuring alternate-form reliability, except that the former is more theoretical and requires a great deal of work, usually by multiple investigators with different approaches.

Divergent

Divergent (discriminant) validity is another theoretically based way of thinking about the ability of a measure to estimate the underlying truth in a given area. For a survey instrument to have divergent validity, it must be shown not to correlate too closely with similar but distinct concepts or traits. This, too, requires much effort over many years of evaluation.

Validity Recap

Testing a survey instrument for construct validity is more like hypothesis testing than like calculating correlation coefficients. Demonstrating construct validity is much more difficult and usually requires a great deal of effort in many different experiments. Construct validity may be said to result from the continued use of a survey instrument to measure some trait, quality, or "construct." Indeed, over a period of years, the survey instrument itself may define the way we think about the variable. It is difficult to present a specific example of construct validity because its measurement and documentation require such an all-encompassing and multifaceted research strategy.

The following table summarizes the types of validity and their characteristics along with comments on their use.

Type of Validity	Characteristics	Comments
Face	Casual review of how good an item or group of items appear	Assessed by individuals with no formal training in the subject under study
Content	Formal expert review of how good an item or series of items appears	Usually assessed by individuals with expertise in some aspect of the subject under study
Criterion: Concurrent	Measures how well the item or scale correlates with "gold standard" measures of the same variable	Requires the identification of an established, generally accepted gold standard
Criterion: Predictive	Measures how well the item or scale predicts expected future observations	Used to predict outcomes or events of significance that the item or scale might subsequently be used to predict
Construct	Theoretical measure of how meaningful a survey instrument is	Determined usually after years of experience by numerous investigators

Validity is usually expressed as a correlation coefficient, or *r* value, between two sets of data. Levels of 0.70 or more are generally accepted as representing good validity.

4 Scaling and Scoring

Scales and indexes are not merely collections of reliable and valid items about the same topic. In fact, most established scales represent months or years of work at refining the list of items down to the critical ones that provide a rich view of a single attribute. The most common method used to assess whether different items belong together in a scale is a technique called **factor analysis.** A factor is a hypothesized trait that is thought to be measured with items in a scale. In factor analysis, a computer-executed algorithm is used to test many different possible combinations of items to determine which of them vary together. Factor analysis is used to evaluate and select items from a larger pool for inclusion in a scale or index. The resulting scale is used to produce a score, which in turn is thought to reflect the factor. The factor itself is a theoretical trait or attribute that is only approximated by the scale. Another advanced computer-executed technique called **multitrait scaling analysis** is sometimes used to measure how well a group of items holds together as a scale.

Example 4.1 provides an illustration of how factor analysis might be used to select items for a scale that purports to measure viewer hostility toward sportscasters during Olympic broadcasts.

EXAMPLE 4.1
Factor Analysis of Olympic Sportscasters

Bryant works for United Broadcasting Company (UBC) and wishes to measure television viewer hostility toward the sportscasters at Good Broadcasting System (GBS) during its Winter Olympics coverage. Bryant knows that viewer hostility will be a difficult concept to define, measure, and package into a scale. He begins by administering a reliable 100-item survey to 350 adult viewers on 10 nights of television coverage of the Winter Olympics. The questions cover a wide range of viewer responses, including pleasure, boredom, anger, identification with athletes, patriotism, and exasperation.

After the Games are over, Bryant compiles all his data and enters them into the mainframe computer at UBC. He performs a factor analysis, in which he hypothesizes which items will measure his trait of interest—hostility—and various other traits that the survey might measure. The computer puts out a matrix of statistics, or factor analysis, that examines how well the items hypothesized to measure hostility vary with each other and how well or poorly they vary with the other hypothesized traits. Of the 12 items he has selected, Bryant's factor analysis determines that only 7 of them vary together well enough to form a hostility scale. The other 5 turn out to vary more closely with other hypothesized traits. Bryant presents his hostility scale to the president of UBC, who must decide how to use it against GBS during negotiations for the exclusive rights to cover the upcoming Summer Olympic Games.

One popular way to structure response sets in survey research is called the *Likert scale* method. It involves a series of typically 5 statements that convey various levels of agreement with an item stem. For example, the survey instructions might ask respondents to state how much they agree with the statement "The hotel guest services were satisfactory," using a set of Likert scale responses that reads "strongly agree," "somewhat agree," "neither agree nor disagree," "somewhat disagree," or "strongly disagree." Another item might read "How often do you feel your self-esteem is low?" and uses a Likert scale response set that reads "All of the time," "much of the time," "about half the time," "some of the time," or "none of the time." There are numerous other ways to structure response sets, which are discussed more fully in **How to Ask Survey Questions** (Vol. 2 in this series).

Scoring a survey instrument is usually fairly straightforward and amenable to the creation of computer-driven algorithms. Most established survey instruments have published scoring manuals that instruct the user on how many points to count for each response to each item. It is important to read the scoring rules carefully because many variations exist on how to convert raw scores to standardized scale scores. This allows the researcher to compare different populations from different studies. In some survey instruments, a high score is better; in others, a high score is worse. Some are converted to a standard 0 to 100 range, whereas others may use a range that goes from 0 to 1, 4, 25, and so forth.

When creating a set of scoring rules for your new survey instrument, you must determine whether to use a sum, an average, or some other formula to derive the scale score. Because different items may have different response options, you must decide whether to value each response or each item the same.

Example 4.2 shows how using different scoring techniques can produce very different survey results from the same data.

EXAMPLE 4.2
Scoring of a Beach Quality Index

To select a site for next year's beachfront intramural volleyball tournament, Morgan and Kim design a new two-item index that measures the quality of different beaches. The two items and number of points for each response are as follows:

Circle one number for each item

1. The average summer temperature at this beach is:

    < 70° 0
    70° to 80° 1
    > 80° 2

2. The average number of clear days per summer month at this beach is:

    < 7 0
    7 to 13 1
    14 to 20 2
    21 to 25 3
    > 25 4

After extensive testing of reliability and validity at various sample beaches, they are happy with the survey instrument. However, they disagree on how to carry out the scoring. Morgan wants to score the index by summing the number of points for both items, dividing by 6 (the perfect score for both items), and then reporting the result. Kim wants to score the index by calculating the percentage score for each of the two items and then averaging them together. Kim would divide the number of points in Item 1 by 2 (a perfect score for that item), divide the number of points in Item 2 by 4 (a perfect score for that item), and then calculate a mean score for the two items. Both scores would be reported on a 100-point scale, but they would be calculated differently. To see whether there is a difference in the two methods, they convince the tournament administrator to fly them to Cape Cod, Massachusetts, for a trial.

While on Cape Cod, Morgan and Kim travel to Provincetown and rate the beach at Race Point with scores of 2 and 3, respectively, for the two items. By Morgan's scoring method, Race Point would score $(2 + 3)/6 = 83\%$. By Kim's method, Race Point would score $[(2/2) + (3/4)]/2 = 88\%$.

The reason why Kim's method yields a higher score is that both items are valued equally by scoring them individually and averaging the item results. Race Point has a perfect score on Item 1, so Kim's method values Item 1 more highly. Morgan's method values each item response, not each item, equally. Therefore, the responses in Item 1 are relatively discounted in the total score.

Example 4.2 shows us that seemingly subtle alterations in scoring methods can lead to significant differences in scale scores. Both Morgan's and Kim's methods are correct, but they place different values on the items. When designing a scoring system for a new survey instrument, you must recognize these differences and plan accordingly. Remember, if you score a scale by simply adding up the total number of points from each item, those items with larger response sets will be valued relatively higher than those with smaller response sets. One way of avoiding this problem and valuing all responses equally is to assign increased points to each response in items with smaller response sets. This common technique is demonstrated in Example 4.3.

EXAMPLE 4.3
Beach Quality Revisited

After much discussion, Kim wins the scoring debate with Morgan, and they decide to score their two-item Beach Quality Index in a manner that confers equal weight to each item. The scoring system they produce is this:

	Response	Points Counted
Item 1	0	0
	1	25
	2	50
Item 2	0	0
	1	12.5
	2	25
	3	37.5
	4	50

With this method, scoring is accomplished simply by summing the number of assigned points for each response. Race Point, the beach from Example 4.2, would be scored by adding 50 (Item 1 = 2) and 37.5 (Item 2 = 3) to yield a score of 87.5, which is rounded to 88%—the exact same answer as Kim obtained in Example 4.2.

5 Creating and Using a Codebook

In survey research, coding is the process of going through each respondent's questionnaire and looking for conflicting answers, missing data, handwritten notes, and other variations from the desired "circle one answer" responses. Before recording your survey responses onto a data tape or into a computer file for analysis, you must decide how you are going to categorize the ambiguous answers. No matter how clearly you spell out the instructions to circle only one answer for each item, you will have unclear responses to some items. It may be that the respondent does not correctly follow instructions for your skip patterns or that the respondent circles more than one answer in a response set that is supposed to be mutually exclusive and collectively exhaustive. No matter how thoroughly you think through your items and response sets before testing your survey, there will always be issues that arise during data collection that require you to make subjective decisions or corrections.

Example 5.1 shows one issue that came up during a recent survey of family support systems.

EXAMPLE 5.1
How Many Kids?

In a recent self-administered survey of family support systems in men with emphysema, one seemingly straightforward question caused a moderate amount of confusion in several respondents. The item read:

Circle one number for this item

How many of your children under age 18 live in your home?

None..............	0
1	1
2 to 4	2
More than 4	3

Three respondents answered *none* but wrote in the margin that 2 to 4 of their wives' school-aged children from previous marriages lived in the home. During the coding of this survey, the researchers decided to count the wives' young children because stepchildren in the home fulfilled a role similar enough to biological children that there should be no distinction in this study. The research context determined how these children were classified. If the same item had appeared on a survey assessing male fertility, it would not have been appropriate to include the stepchildren. This decision was recorded in the study's codebook for future reference.

   The most common data problem is that respondents will skip items either intentionally or by mistake. Usually, you will have to code those items as missing data and decide later how to treat them in the analysis. Occasionally, you can infer the answer to an item from other responses or from other sources, particularly if it is a sociodemographic item, such as age. The best way to handle missing data is to call the respondent and ask for the correct answer to the skipped item. However, this is not always possible. Example 5.2 demonstrates one way to solve the problem of missing data.

EXAMPLE 5.2
Missing Data

In the same survey of family support systems in men with emphysema, the researchers included the following item on family outings:

Circle one number for this item

During the past 4 weeks, how often did you and *all* the other family members who live in your home go out to dinner together?

Not at all.	0
Once or twice	1
Three to five times.	2
Six or more times.	3

After all the surveys had been returned, they were coded by an undergraduate student research assistant, who found that 15 respondents had failed to answer this item. When he reported this to the study's principal investigator, she asked him to telephone these 15 respondents to try to fill in the missing data. Nine were available and provided answers to this item, but 6 were not reachable despite numerous attempts. The telephone follow-up was also recorded in the study codebook for future reference.

Example 5.2 illustrates that missing data is one of the most problematic areas in survey research. It is critically important to make extensive efforts to minimize the amount of missing data from a survey. Missing data detract from the overall quality of the survey results. They also serve as a quality check on the research methods: The more data that are missing, the poorer the quality of the methodology. Data may be missing for a variety of reasons. Respondents may omit data because they misunderstood skip patterns, failed to grasp the language used, were unable to read the type, tired of a lengthy survey, or for many other reasons. Whatever the explanation, missing data can be devastating to an otherwise well-planned survey project.

In Example 5.3, the value of the codebook is demonstrated when a surveyor makes a decision regarding data after the data had been collected but before they were coded on the survey.

EXAMPLE 5.3
Counting Homicides

Alison, the president of the National Gay and Lesbian Media Coalition (NGLMC), performed a survey to review all articles appearing in daily newspapers in the 50 largest cities in North America during the last 3 years). One of the variables she collected was the number of articles with positive coverage of gay and lesbian issues in each city during each year. She found the article counts to range from none to 455. During the data collection stage of her project, Alison decided to enter the exact number of articles on a blank line next to the question. Later, when she coded the surveys, she decided to collapse the article counts into six groups, which she felt were more meaningful:

Number of Articles	Response Code
0	1
1 to 10	2
11 to 50	3
51 to 174	4
175 to 350	5
> 350	6

Alison made a research decision that she did not need to analyze her data based on the exact number of articles. She recorded the above table in her study codebook for future reference. She knew that if she decided to add more cities to her series several years later, she would not be able to remember where she had drawn the lines between groups. She also knew that her thorough codebook would provide that information.

In some senses, the codebook is a log or documentation of the research decisions that are made during the coding or review of surveys. Despite your best efforts, you will be unable to remember all the small decisions that you make along the way in carrying out the collection, processing, and analysis of survey data. The codebook is a summary of all those decisions. It functions not only as a record but also as a rule book for future analyses with the same or similar data.

The importance of keeping meticulous records cannot be overemphasized. Inevitably in survey research, questions arise about how you collected a data element, where you went for resources, how you documented certain variables, or whether you completed follow-up in a certain way. The only way to guarantee that you can reproduce your methods accurately is to maintain excellent records. This includes your codebook and the way you structured each aspect of your methodology and data analysis.

6 Pilot Testing

Before a new feature film appears in movie theaters, movie studios always show it to sample audiences in various cities to observe their reactions to the characters, plot, ending, and other aspects of the entertainment experience. If some aspect of the film is consistently disliked by these sample audiences, it is usually changed before the movie is released. Similarly, before a new product is introduced into retail stores, manufacturers always test market it to gauge consumer satisfaction. And before buying a new car, you almost always take it for a test drive, even if you are already certain about your choice of models.

Likewise in survey research, one of the most important stages in the development of a new survey instrument involves trying it out on a small sample population. **Pilot testing,** or pretesting, your questionnaire will time and again prove to be worth your energy. Pilot testing almost always identifies errors in a survey's form and presentation. Inevitably, despite extensive thought and planning, errors occur in the final versions of questionnaires. They range from confusing typographical mistakes to overlapping response sets to ambiguous instructions. Usually, the authors are so close to the project that they may overlook even the most obvious of errors. Pilot testing allows the authors a chance to correct these errors before the survey is mass produced or used on a wider scope to gather real data. It allows authors the time and opportunity to redesign problematic parts of the survey before it is actually used. Pilot testing also predicts difficulties that may arise during subsequent data collection that might otherwise have gone unnoticed. At this early stage, most problems are still correctable.

Sometimes, the issues identified during pilot testing are problems of form. For older individuals, many of whom have impaired vision, the type size and font are especially important. Difficulties may also arise with reading comprehension. Many survey respondents are less technically educated than survey researchers. If a survey is written at a level beyond the understanding of its respondents, the resulting data will be spurious or incomplete. Respondents must be able to understand the semantics of the survey items in order to provide honest and thoughtful answers. Likewise, many populations today are not homogeneous in their primary language. Even if a survey is written at a comprehensible level, individuals who are not completely fluent or comfortable with English may answer with data that are not usable.

Language may present significant challenges; however, just because your respondents are not fluent English speakers does not mean you cannot gather data from them. If you are very industrious, you may actually create a foreign-language version of your survey if there is information that you want but is only reliably and validly available in the respondents' native tongue.

In addition, items must be culturally sensitive. Certain areas that are covered in a questionnaire may represent concepts that are unfamiliar to individuals involved in the survey. A more thorough discussion of this potential trap is included in the next chapter. Pilot testing allows many potential impediments to be identified and corrected in advance before too many resources have been expended. You must be careful to avoid these pitfalls when crossing language and cultural barriers in survey research (see Chapter 7 on multicultural issues). Pilot testing will not eliminate any of these problems, but it will identify them so that the researcher can consider the implications and decide prospectively how to handle them.

Example 6.1 demonstrates one of the simple but common problems that is identified when pilot-testing a survey.

EXAMPLE 6.1
Type Size

Ramon was very pleased that his new 10-item questionnaire on attitudes toward aging fits onto one side of a single page. He estimated that it should require about 5 minutes to complete. Before assessing his survey's reliability and validity in a sample of 125 older New Yorkers, Ramon was urged by his professor to conduct a small pilot test with 6 senior citizens. Ramon set up the pilot test by calling the activities office of a local community center and recruiting volunteers.

On the appointed date, the 4 women and 2 men met Ramon at the community center for the short pilot test. To his surprise, Ramon found that the average time they took to complete his survey was 10 minutes. When he queried them as to why, 5 of the 6 stated that they had a great deal of trouble reading the questions, even with their glasses. They had no problems with reading comprehension or with English; they simply could not read the type on the page.

Ramon revised the type size on his survey from 8-point to 12-point type. Instead of fitting onto a single page, the survey now took up two pages. Ramon mailed the new version to his 6 pilot-test respondents and asked for their comments. Each of them replied that it was now much easier to read and complete.

When designing questionnaire layout, authors are often tempted to squeeze as many items as possible onto one or two pages. They think that if a survey looks shorter, it will be easier and quicker to complete. But shortening the length of a questionnaire by making the type size smaller only makes it more difficult to read. If respondents have trouble reading the words on the page, they will not have much energy left to think about the meaning of the questions. Ramon learned in Example 6.1 that sometimes a survey that is a few more pages in length but much easier to read can yield more valuable results than one that fits nicely into a short format. If the type is easier to read, it takes less time to complete two pages than one.

One trick that some researchers have used is creative numbering of the items. Instead of simply numbering questions from 1 to whatever, breaking items into groups or sections may create the illusion that a survey is shorter than it really is. If several items in a survey rely on the same response set, you can turn them into a single item with instructions to circle the column of the correct response. Rather than numbering each item separately, you number the instruction and define the items with letters. This technique is demonstrated in Example 6.2.

EXAMPLE 6.2
Arizona Geological Survey

Eric wishes to collect data on the types of rocks found in the various counties of Arizona. He designs a 40-item questionnaire to be completed by the interior commissioner of each county, but he knows that these individuals are quite busy and may not want to take the time to complete a lengthy survey. After some basic research, Eric discovers that the three most common rock forms in the state are quartz, limestone, and clay. Before sending out his survey, Eric performs a pilot test with two of the commissioners he knows personally. Their main complaint is that 40 items seem like quite a lot. Because Eric does not want to delete any of the items, he revises the numbering system of his survey and mails out his survey.

In his cover letter, Eric introduces his research project and asks for the commissioners' help in complying with a "short 10-item survey." Eric crafts a survey format that relies heavily on grouping similar items together. His first six items are grouped as follows:

Please circle the number corresponding to the most common type of rock at these sites in your county.

	Quartz	Limestone	Clay
Lakes	1	2	3
Hills	1	2	3
Mountains	1	2	3
Suburbs	1	2	3
Forests	1	2	3
Riverbeds	1	2	3

By combining his items together into groups, as shown above, Eric is able to reduce 40 items to 10 items without shortening his survey at all. It simply appears shorter. Eric hopes to find that despite their busy schedules, the county interior commissioners will be cooperative in completing his "short" questionnaire.

Surveys do not have to be filled with page after page of boring and monotonous questions. You can spice up the demeanor of your survey instrument by using some very simple techniques. Varying the response sets into columns for like groups, as in Example 6.2, is one commonly used method. Another is the incorporation of graphics into the response sets. After a series of difficult questions, you can place a few short easy questions to provide a mental break for the respondent.

Another difficulty that presents challenges for survey researchers is how to design skip patterns. The instruction "If you answered yes to the previous question, then skip to page 4" may be a wonderful way to use the same questionnaire for different groups, but it may cause you and your respondents untold frustration. Often, pilot testing will identify this type of simple visual problem with your survey's layout and format. At this stage, it can easily be corrected and retested before proceeding to your primary effort at data collection.

Example 6.3 illustrates the problem of the confusing skip pattern, a difficulty that is often identified during pilot testing. At this early stage, it is easily corrected, but if it appeared in the actual survey it could lead to devastating amounts of missing data.

EXAMPLE 6.3
Algebra Attitudes

Kathleen wishes to survey the attitudes of Chicago ninth graders toward different approaches to learning math. She designs a comprehensive questionnaire with several branch points that direct students to different sets of questions. The first item in the questionnaire is as follows:

Circle one letter for Item 1

1. Would you prefer to learn algebra by:

   Listening to a teacher present new material
   and working problems . . . .   A

   Listening to a teacher but working problems
   on your own . . . .   B

   Reading new material and working problems
   all on your own   C

If you answered A, continue with Item 2-11 but skip Items 12-36 and then complete Items 37-50. If you answered B, skip Items 2-11, continue with Items 12-23, skip Items 24-36, and complete Items 37-50. If you answered C, skip Items 2-23 but complete Items 24-50.

Before taking her survey into the entire school district, Kathleen pilot-tested it in her daughter's ninth-grade class of 30 girls and boys. She found that the students had numerous questions about the skip patterns. Despite their best efforts, the instructions were simply too confusing for them. Kathleen was forced to take her survey back to the drawing board to make it more "user friendly" for these respondents. In her revision, she used graphic images and hand-drawn arrows to direct students through the skip patterns more easily. When she returned to the same class to repeat her pilot test, she found that the students sailed through it without any apparent difficulty.

Pilot testing is not limited to new survey instruments. It is beneficial in even the most well-established survey instruments. Unless you are working with a population that is exactly the same as those in which a survey instrument has been validated, you will probably be introducing some new twist in your particular sample. Pilot testing established survey instruments is extraordinarily helpful in all survey research. You may find for whatever reason that even an established survey instrument does not perform well in your sample. This will afford you the opportunity to select a different survey instrument or even develop your own if you have the time and resources.

Example 6.4 demonstrates another potential problem often identified during pilot testing: the issue of item nonrelevance in your population.

EXAMPLE 6.4
Type A Personalities

The Jenkins Activity Scale is a published and well-established survey instrument that distinguishes individuals with relatively high levels of daily anxiety and compulsion, so-called Type A personalities, from those with lower levels of stress, so-called Type B personalities. It was intended to identify people at risk for heart attacks, strokes, and high blood pressure.

In an effort to find potential clients with certain investment habits, a money management firm decided to mail out this self-administered survey to a national sample of 5,000 members of the American Association of Retired Persons (AARP). The firm has an idea that Type B personalities are more likely to hand over their savings for investments without asking too many questions. After a thorough literature review, the firm's marketing department selected the Jenkins Activity Survey because it was short, easily scored, and well documented to be reliable and valid. The marketing director submitted his proposal to the firm's vice president for growth.

Before committing the firm's resources to this particular survey instrument, the vice president asked her assistant to conduct a small pilot test of the Jenkins Activity Survey with 12 members of the local AARP chapter. Of the 8 surveys that were returned, 7 respondents completed only a small fraction of the items. It turned out that most of the items on the survey referred to respondents' conduct at work, interactions with professional colleagues, and number of vacation days taken from the job. Of the 8 people who replied to the pilot test, only 1 was currently employed. The remainder were retired and could not answer, not surprising given the target audience of retired persons.

The vice president fired the marketing director and hired an expensive outside consulting firm to develop and psychometrically evaluate a new survey instrument that assesses daily anxiety levels in retired persons as a predictor of investment strategies.

Pilot testing is a necessary and important part of survey development. It provides useful information about how your survey instrument actually plays in the field. Although it requires extra time and energy, the pilot test is a critical step in assessing the practical application of your survey instrument.

Checklist for Pilot Testing

✓ Are there any typographical errors?

✓ Are there any misspelled words?

✓ Do the item numbers make sense?

✓ Is the type size big enough to be easily read?

✓ Is the vocabulary appropriate for the respondents?

✓ Is the survey too long?

✓ Is the style of the items too monotonous?

✓ Are there easy questions in with the difficult questions?

✓ Are the skip patterns too difficult?

✓ Does the survey format flow well?

✓ Are the items appropriate for the respondents?

✓ Are the items sensitive to possible cultural barriers?

✓ Is the survey in the best language for the respondents?

7 Multicultural Issues

When designing new survey instruments or applying established ones in populations of different ethnicity, creed, or nationality, you must make sure that your items translate well into both the language and the culture of your target audience. Although you may be able to translate a survey instrument's items into a new language, they may not measure the same dimension in that culture. This is particularly relevant when studying social attitudes and health behaviors. Different cultures have very different concepts of health, well-being, illness, and disease, for example. Therefore, a well-developed concept in one culture may not even exist in another. Even if you start with a well-validated survey instrument in English, various populations within the United States and

69

elsewhere in the world may not approach the concept with the same ideas.

Failing to be attentive to multicultural issues may result in significant bias when collecting data. For example, when classifying ethnicities, survey researchers often categorize all Asians together. For some projects, this may be acceptable; however, many attitudes and behaviors vary tremendously among Chinese, Japanese, Thai, Vietnamese, and other cultures within Asia. By blithely lumping them all into one class, you may overlook differences that are important to your conclusions.

Example 7.1 shows that problems can arise not only from language barriers but also from conceptual differences due to culture.

EXAMPLE 7.1
Elderly Women

Olivia decided to use an established, well-validated, 24-item survey instrument to measure family attitudes in elderly American women of Anglo and Latina descent. To facilitate crossing the potential language barrier, she asked her girlfriend, a native Mexican, to translate the survey into Spanish. After the translation was complete, Olivia administered it to a sample of 300 elderly women, of whom 150 classified themselves as Latina and 150 classified themselves as Anglo-American.

After tabulating her data, Olivia was disappointed to discover that, despite the perfect translation into Spanish, a tremendous amount of data was missing from the Latina respondents' surveys. When she researched the matter more closely, Olivia realized that she had failed to take into account the multicultural issues raised by her project. She found out that the Latina women had a concept of family that was completely different from that of the Anglo-Americans. For example, the Anglos tended to include only parents and children in their concept of family, whereas the Latinas tended to also include grandparents, aunts and uncles, and cousins. The survey instrument had been validated only in Anglo-American populations. Although the words in the survey had been translated quite well into Spanish, the modern philosophy of family in the two groups were so different that most of the Anglo concepts had no real meaning for the Latinas. Therefore, they left many items blank, and Olivia was unable to analyze her data in a useful way.

Exercises

1. Northwest Cable administers a television preference survey to 100 viewers in its southeastern region and presents the following two items at different points in the same survey:

   - How many hours of TV did you watch in the past 7 days?

   - How many programs of what length did you watch during the past 7 days?

   The company is trying to document

   a. Alternate form reliability

   b. Test-retest reliability

   c. Internal consistency reliability

   d. All of the above

2. If Southwest Cable administers a new television preference questionnaire to 50 viewers in its northeastern region on January 15, then repeats the identical survey with the same 50 viewers on February 15, and finds close correlations between the two data sets, its survey instrument can be said to have good

   a. Alternate form reliability

   b. Test-retest reliability

   c. Internal consistency reliability

   d. All of the above

3. When you read that a scale has a coefficient alpha of 0.90, you can be assured that the scale has a high degree of

   a. Alternate form reliability

   b. Test-retest reliability

   c. Internal consistency reliability

   d. All of the above

4. If you were developing a measure of student satisfaction with school lunches in a 750-student elementary school, how might you design an experiment to assess test-retest reliability?

5. Design two different response sets to test alternate-form reliability for the following item from a meteorological survey instrument about regional precipitation:

> *How much rain did your region*
> *have during the past 4 weeks?*

6. A new survey instrument is published for assessing safety in automobiles. It contains 12 items about a wide range of qualities, such as strength of the seatbelt straps, temperature at which the engine overheats, how well the windshield shatters

during impact, thickness of the steel in the doors, and adequacy of the ventilation system. After the survey instrument is tested in several models, it is determined that the instrument has good test-retest and alternate-form reliability, but its coefficient alpha is only 0.23. What does this mean?

7. The housing office of a large university wants to measure student satisfaction with various aspects of the campus dormitories. After researching the relevant published literature, the housing director cannot find a survey instrument that she thinks is appropriate, so she decides to develop her own. She remembers from her survey research course in college that her index must be reliable and valid. She also remembers that her index must have good content validity. How would you advise her to begin her project?

8. Brian has designed and pilot-tested a new 20-item, self-administered survey instrument that measures religious observance in a group of Midwesterners. How might he go about assessing it for concurrent validity?

9. Obsessions Unlimited is a company that provides personal organization services for individuals who pay a fee in return for individual help in organizing their personal lives. The company is looking for a better way to assess the quality of its applicants for employment as personal organization assistants. The director of personnel wants to devise a screening questionnaire that has excellent predictive validity in selecting assistants who will produce customer satisfaction. He puts together a reliable self-administered index of 20 items, which can be easily completed by applicants for the job. How should he test his index's predictive validity?

ANSWERS

1. Alternate-form reliability

2. Test-retest reliability

3. Internal consistency reliability

4. Because satisfaction with the lunches may be different on any given day, you must administer your survey at separate times on the same afternoon after the lunch in question. For example, you might have students complete a questionnaire right after they return from lunch and again right before school lets out.

5. *Response Set 1:* In this region, the average total rainfall (to the nearest 10th of an inch) during the past 4 weeks was:

> None
>
> 0.1 to 4 inches
>
> 4.1 to 8 inches
>
> 8.1 to 12 inches
>
> More than 12 inches

Response Set 2: In this region, the number of days it rained during the past 4 weeks was:

No days

1 to 7 days

8 to 14 days

15 to 21 days

22 to 28 days

Response Set 3: In this region, rainfall during the past 4 weeks has been:

Below average for this time of year

About average for this time of year

Above average for this time of year

6. The survey instrument has low internal consistency reliability. This means that although the items seem to focus on various aspects of the same concept, they may actually be quite different. The author should consider the possibility that the items may not be measuring the same concept.

7. If she wants to ensure content validity, she must tailor her survey instrument to the needs of the students themselves. The best way to start would be to put together a focus group of students presently living in the campus dorms. During this exploratory session, she could get an idea of what issues are important to them. She might then put together a first draft of

her questionnaire and show it to these students for their comments. This would provide initial testing of content validity.

8. To assess concurrent validity, Brian must identify some "gold standard" method of assessing religious observance. He should start by looking in the sociology research literature. Because there may not be such an established measure, he may have to select a measure that appears to be a gold standard. For example, he might use actual attendance at religious services or religious functions during a 4-week period for a randomly selected group of Midwesterners.

9. To test predictive validity of his screening questionnaire, the personnel director must also select an established outcome measure of customer satisfaction. He should administer his questionnaire to all employment applicants over a defined period of time. He should then use the selected outcome measure to document the satisfaction of those customers served by the different employees. By using the results from the screening index to try to predict which employees will have good results on the satisfaction outcomes measure, he can assess the predictive validity of his questionnaire. If those who score well on the screening index also score well on the satisfaction index, then his screening index can be said to have good predictive validity.

Suggested Readings

Fowlern, F. J. (1988). *Survey research methods.* Newbury Park, CA: Sage.

A user-friendly and practical guide to the fundamentals of good survey design.

McDowell, I., & Newell, C. (1987). *Measuring health: A guide to rating scales and questionnaires.* Oxford, UK: Oxford University Press.

A comprehensive guide to the most commonly used health questionnaires, complete with examples of actual items, reliability and validity data, and author addresses for each questionnaire.

Rossi, P. H., Wright, J. D., & Anderson A. B. (1983). *Handbook of survey research.* San Diego, CA: Academic Press, Harcourt Brace Jovanovich.

One of the most complete manuals available on theory, quantitative methods, and practical issues encountered in various aspects of survey research.

Tulsky, D. S. (1990). An introduction to test theory. *Oncology, 4,* 43-48.

A thorough, succinct summary of the principles of reliability and validity illustrated with case examples.

Wilkin, D., Hallam, L., & Doggett, M. (1992). *Measures of need and outcome for primary health care.* Oxford, UK: Oxford University Press.

Includes a comprehensive chapter on methods of measurement that covers reliability, validity, scoring, and other practical aspects of survey evaluation.

Glossary

Alternate-form reliability Measure of survey reproducibility in which a question is worded in two or more different ways and the different versions are compared for consistency in responses.

Codebook Collection of rules developed when translating survey responses into numerical codes for analysis. For example, a codebook might contain a rule on ethnicity that assigns the number 1 to African Americans, 2 to Anglos, 3 to Asians, 4 to Latinos, and so on. Another rule might assign the number 9 to all items for which data is missing. The codebook is a summary of all such rules to be used as a reference during data analysis.

Concurrent validity Measure of survey accuracy in which the results of a new survey or scale are compared with the results from a generally accepted "gold standard" test after both tests are administered to the same group of respondents.

Construct validity Theoretical gestalt-type measure of how meaningful a survey instrument is, usually after many years of experience by numerous investigators in many varied settings.

Content validity Measure of survey accuracy that involves formal review by individuals who are experts in the subject matter of a survey.

Convergent validity Measure of survey accuracy that involves using different tools to obtain information about a particular variable and seeing how well they correlate. Evaluating convergent validity is analogous to measuring alternate-form reliability but with different established instruments rather than different wordings of a single item.

Correlation coefficient Statistical measure of how closely two variables or measures are related to each other. Correlation coefficients are usually calculated and reported as r values.

Criterion validity Measure of survey accuracy that involves comparing it to other tests. Criterion validity may be categorized as convergent or divergent.

Divergent validity Measure of survey accuracy that involves using different tools for obtaining information about similar but discrete variables and seeing if they differ.

Face validity Most casual measure of a survey's accuracy, usually assessed informally by nonexperts.

Factor analysis Computer-assisted method used to assess whether different items on a survey belong together in one scale.

Index (see **scale**)

Internal consistency reliability Measure of survey accuracy that reflects how well different items in a scale vary together when applied to a group of respondents.

Interobserver reliability Reproducibility of a set of observations on one variable made by different observers.

Intraobserver reliability Reproducibility of a set of observations on one variable made by the same observer at different times.

Item Question that appears on a survey or in an index.

Measurement error Degree to which instruments yield data that are incorrect due to the measurement process.

Multitrait scaling analysis Advanced computer-assisted method of measuring how well various items go together in a particular scale (similar to **factor analysis**).

Pilot testing During the development phase of a new survey or instrument, the practice of trying out the new survey or index in a small sample one or more times to see how well the survey works, expose errors, and identify areas of difficulty for respondents.

Practice effect Phenomenon in which a respondent becomes familiar with items on a survey or index taken at several time points. Over time, the individual's responses correlate highly with each other simply because that person is remembering previous answers and not because the variable being measured is unchanged.

Predictive validity Measure of survey accuracy in which an item or scale is correlated with future observations of behavior, survey responses, or other events.

Psychometrics   Science of measuring psychological or qualitative phenomena.

r **value**   Statistic that is used to report correlations. (see **correlation coefficient**)

Random error   Degree to which instruments yield data that are incorrect *not* due to the measurement process, but due to uncontrollable fluctuations in responses.

Reliability   Reproducibility or stability of data or observations. When using a survey or index, one wants to achieve high reliability, implying that the data are highly reproducible.

Scale   Series of items that measures a single variable, trait, or domain.

Scaling   Process in which different items are placed together in a single index that pertains to one variable of interest. Factor analysis and multitrait scaling analysis are often used in this process.

Scoring   Conversion of an individual's survey answers into a numerical value for comparison with those of other individuals or of the same individual at different times.

Split halves method   Technique used to assess alternate-form reliability, in which a large sample is equally divided into two smaller samples, each of which is administered a different form of the same question. The responses of the two samples are compared to each other. (see **alternate-form reliability**)

Survey instrument or **Survey**   Series of items that typically contains several scales. A survey may be self-administered or require a trained interviewer. It may be very long or contain a single item. It may be about issues as personal as sexual dysfunction or as impersonal as rainfall.

Test-retest reliability   Measure of the stability of responses over time in the same group of respondents. Many investigators report test-retest reliability by administering the same survey at two different time points (often 4 weeks apart) to the same group of individuals.

Validity   Assessment of how well a survey or index measures what it is intended to measure.

About the Author

MARK S. LITWIN, MD, MPH, is Assistant Professor of Health Services and Surgery/Urology at the UCLA Schools of Public Health and Medicine, where he is involved in teaching, clinical practice, and medical outcomes research. His MD is from Emory University, and his urology training was done at Harvard Medical School's Brigham and Women's Hospital. His MPH is from UCLA, where he received a Robert Wood Johnson Clinical Scholars Fellowship. He has extensive experience in health services research projects, including health-related quality of life, medical resource use, physician payment systems, and other areas of health policy.